NIMITZ
AIRCRAFT CARRIERS

BY DENNY VON FINN

EPIC

BELLWETHER MEDIA · MINNEAPOLIS, MN

EPIC BOOKS are no ordinary books. They burst with intense action, high-speed heroics, and shadows of the unknown. Are you ready for an Epic adventure?

This edition first published in 2013 by Bellwether Media, Inc.

No part of this publication may be reproduced in whole or in part without written permission of the publisher. For information regarding permission, write to Bellwether Media, Inc., Attention: Permissions Department, 5357 Penn Avenue South, Minneapolis, MN 55419.

Library of Congress Cataloging-in-Publication Data

Von Finn, Denny.
  Nimitz aircraft carriers / by Denny Von Finn.
    p. cm. – (Epic: military vehicles)
  Summary: "Engaging images accompany information about Nimitz aircraft carriers. The combination of high-interest subject matter and light text is intended for students in grades 2 through 7"–Provided by publisher.
  Audience: Ages 6-12.
  Includes bibliographical references and index.
  ISBN 978-1-60014-887-3 (hbk. : alk. paper)
  1. Aircraft carriers–United States–Juvenile literature. 2. Nimitz Class (Aircraft carriers)–Juvenile literature. I. Title.
  V874.3.V66 2013
  623.825'5–dc23
                    2012038167

Printed in the United States of America, North Mankato, MN.

The photographs in this book are reproduced through the courtesy of the United States Department of Defense.

TABLE OF CONTENTS

Nimitz Aircraft Carriers 4

Crew and Weapons 10

Nimitz Missions 16

Glossary 22

To Learn More 23

Index 24

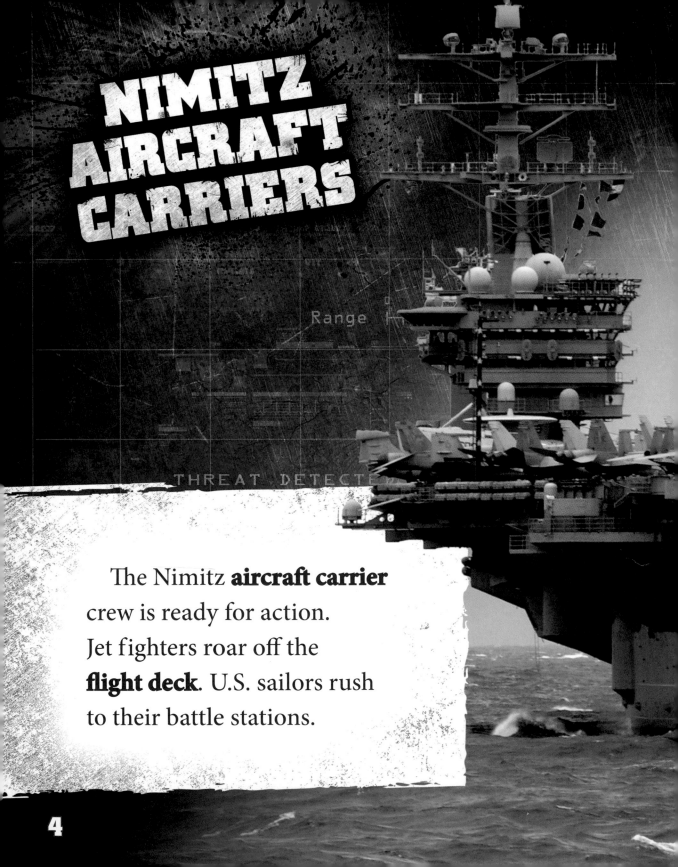

NIMITZ AIRCRAFT CARRIERS

The Nimitz **aircraft carrier** crew is ready for action. Jet fighters roar off the **flight deck**. U.S. sailors rush to their battle stations.

An alarm sounds. An enemy aircraft has slipped past the carrier's jet fighters. The carrier must protect the **strike group**.

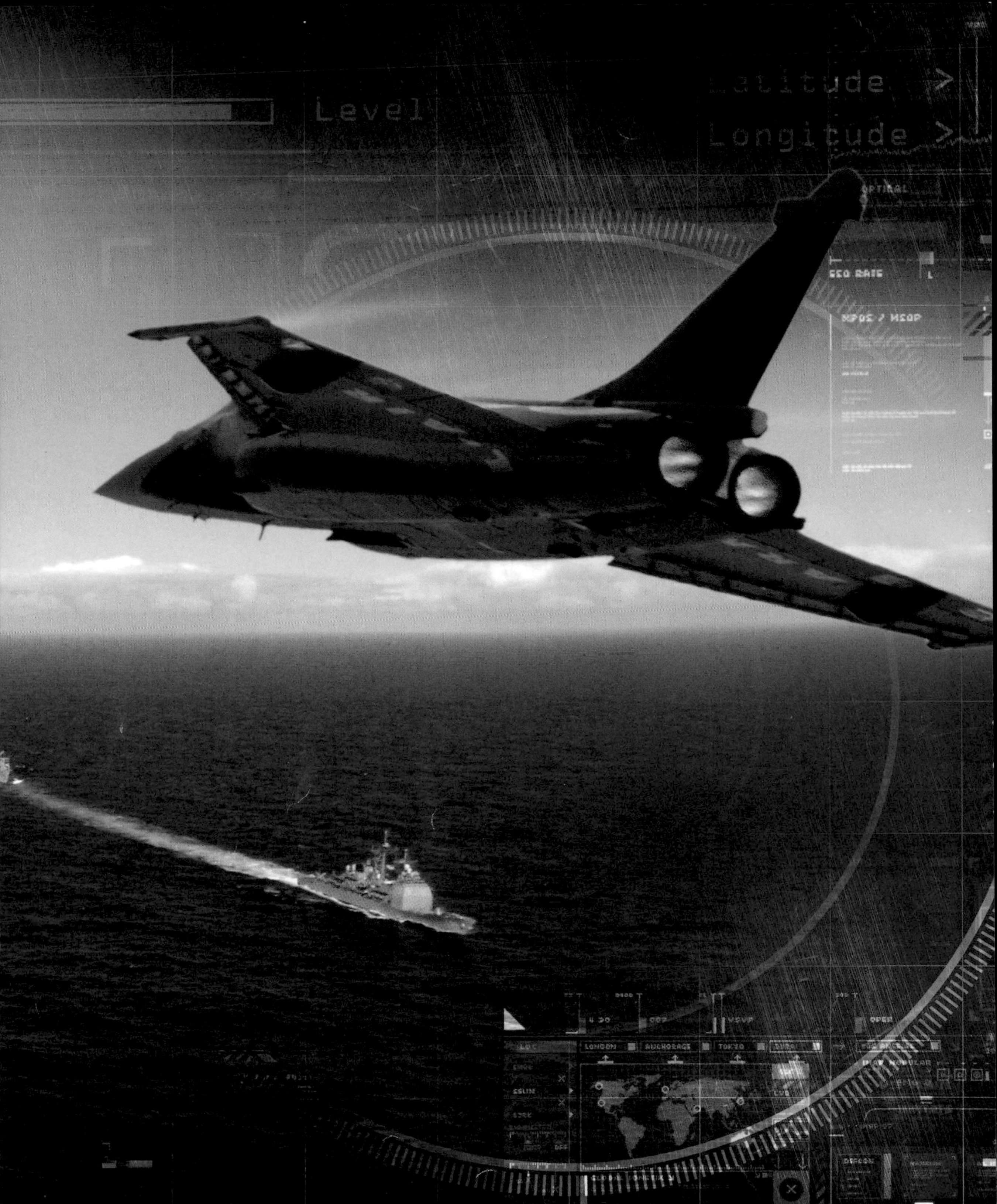
Level
Longitude >
LONDON
ANCHORAGE
TOKYO
OPEN

The Nimitz crew fires a **missile**. The enemy aircraft crashes into the sea. Another **mission** is complete!

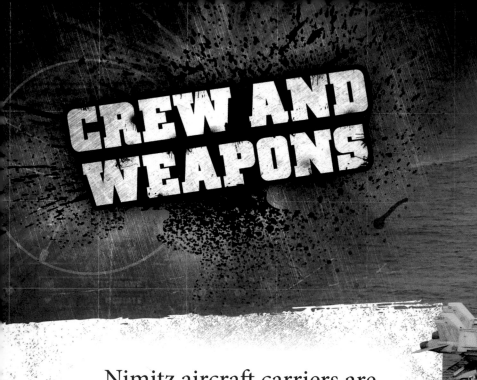

CREW AND WEAPONS

Nimitz aircraft carriers are the world's largest warships. More than 6,000 people can live onboard. They stay in **quarters** below deck.

Nimitz Fact

The flight deck of a Nimitz is longer than three football fields.

Aircraft are the most important weapons on a Nimitz carrier. They are kept in **hangars** below deck.

HANGAR

Nimitz Fact

A Nimitz carrier can have more than 80 aircraft onboard.

The Nimitz carries other weapons for defense. Missiles and cannons keep enemies away.

MISSILE

Nimitz Fact

Nimitz aircraft carriers
are named after Chester W.
Nimitz. He was a U.S. Navy
commander in World War II.

CANNON

NIMITZ MISSIONS

Nimitz carriers perform many missions. They stop enemies from attacking **allies**. They also protect other U.S. ships and help people in need.

Nimitz Fact

A Nimitz aircraft carrier could travel nonstop for more than 20 years without refueling.

Nimitz carriers played a major role in the **War on Terror**. They also delivered food and water to **victims** of **Hurricane Katrina**.

VEHICLE BREAKDOWN:
NIMITZ AIRCRAFT CARRIER

Used By:	**U.S. Navy**
Entered Service:	**1975**
Length:	**1,092 feet (333 meters)**
Flight Deck Width:	**252 feet (76.8 meters)**
Speed:	**more than 34.5 miles (55.5 kilometers) per hour**
Crew:	**about 6,000**
Weapons:	**aircraft, missiles, cannons**
Primary Missions:	**stop enemies, protect U.S. and allied ships, deliver aid**

Ten Nimitz aircraft carriers serve the United States Navy. Their weapons and brave crews help defend countries around the world.

0   50

GLOSSARY

aircraft carrier—a large ship that aircraft can take off from and land on

allies—friendly nations that have common goals or purposes; the United States has many allies around the world.

flight deck—the large, flat surface on top of an aircraft carrier; aircraft take off from and land on the flight deck.

hangars—large rooms where aircraft are stored and repaired

Hurricane Katrina—a deadly hurricane that hit the southeastern United States in 2005; a hurricane is a spinning rainstorm that starts over warm ocean waters.

missile—an explosive that is guided to a target

mission—a military task

quarters—the areas of a ship where sailors live

strike group—a group of several war and supply ships that travel together

victims—people who are hurt, killed, or made to suffer

War on Terror—a war led by the United States to stop organized groups from performing acts of violence; the War on Terror began in 2001.

TO LEARN MORE

At the Library

Doeden, Matt. *Aircraft Carriers*. Mankato, Minn.: Capstone Press, 2005.

Zobel, Derek. *Nimitz Aircraft Carriers*. Minneapolis, Minn.: Bellwether Media, 2009.

Zuehlke, Jeffrey. *Warships*. Minneapolis, Minn.: Lerner Publications Co., 2006.

On the Web

Learning more about Nimitz aircraft carriers is as easy as 1, 2, 3.

1. Go to www.factsurfer.com.

2. Enter "Nimitz aircraft carriers" into the search box.

3. Click the "Surf" button and you will see a list of related Web sites.

With factsurfer.com, finding more information is just a click away.

INDEX

aircraft, 6, 9, 12, 13, 19

allies, 17, 19

cannons, 14, 15, 19

crew, 4, 9, 10, 19, 21

flight deck, 4, 10, 12, 19

hangars, 12, 13

Hurricane Katrina, 18

jet fighters, 4, 6

missiles, 9, 14, 19

missions, 9, 17, 19

Nimitz, Chester W., 15

quarters, 10

range, 17

strike group, 6

United States Navy, 15, 19, 21

War on Terror, 18